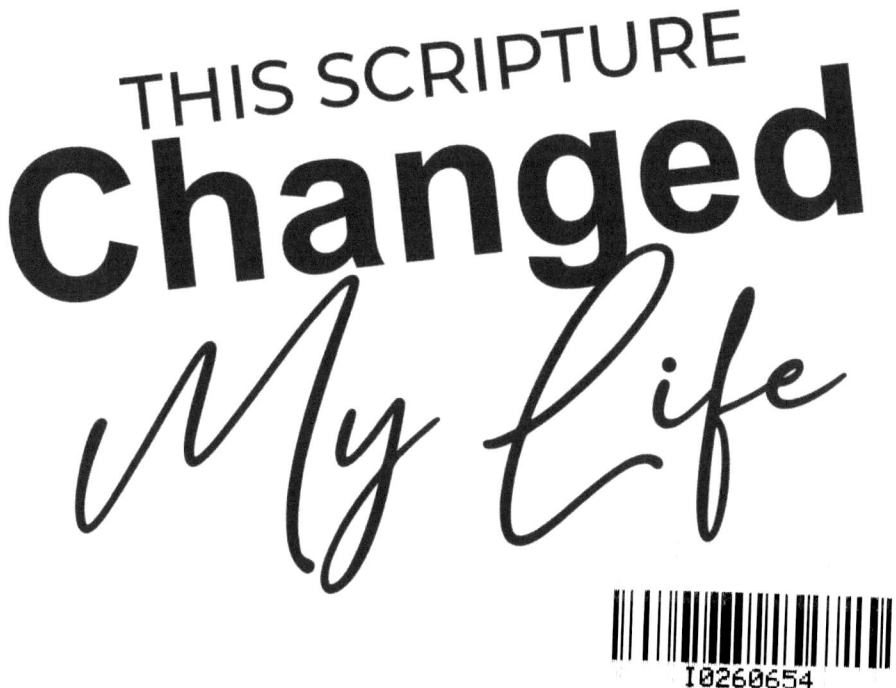

AMY PHILPOTT | DEBORAH FRANKLIN | ERICA QUARLES
ETHEL J. DAVIS | JACKIE "LADY J" MILLER | PIXIE LEE
TRACY SHORTER | WENDY DAILEY | DR. YVETTE HARRIS

©2024 by Deborah Franklin Publishing (DFP)

All rights are reserved. No portion of this book may be reproduced, stored in a retrieval system, or transmitted in any form or by any means- electronic, mechanical, photocopy, recording, scanning, or other - except for brief quotations in critical reviews or articles, without the prior written permission of the above publishers.

ISBN 979-8-9875656-7-4

Purpose

The purpose of *This Scripture Changed My Life* is to showcase the profound and transformative power of scripture through real-life experiences. By sharing the stories of women who have turned to specific Bible verses for guidance, comfort, and empowerment during pivotal moments in their lives, the book aims to:

1. Inspire: Highlight how faith can be a powerful source of strength and resilience in the face of life's challenges, offering readers hope and encouragement in their own struggles.
2. Empower: Demonstrate the practical application of scripture in everyday life, showing how verses can provide direction and support when navigating difficult circumstances.
3. Guide: Offer readers insights into how they might use scripture as a tool for personal growth and transformation, encouraging them to find their own meaningful verses.
4. Comfort: Provide solace and reassurance by illustrating that others have faced similar trials and found peace through their faith, fostering a sense of connection and shared experience.

Overall, the book seeks to be a source of motivation, inspiration and spiritual enrichment, helping readers see the tangible impact of faith in action.

Table of Contents

Purpose ii

The Gift 1
    Deborah Franklin 4

Unleash the Revolution of Protection Through Disaster 8
    Erica Quarles 10

Empty Vessels, Fulfilled Blessings 14
    Amy Philpott 18

My Plan vs. God's Plan 22
    Pixie Lee 25

Entering His Rest 30
    Wendy Dailey 34

Who am I, and where did I come from? 37
    Ethel J. Davis 42

"Trusting in God's Providential Care" 46
    Jacqueline B. Miller 51

Broadening Your Perspective 56
    Dr. Yvette Harris 60

Committing to His Plan through your Pain 65
   Tracy D. Shorter 69

The Gift

By Deborah Franklin

Walking around in a daze not knowing where I belonged or what my future may hold and being the child that was different who rather read a book or write in her journal didn't quite fit in the sports driven family that God placed me in. Never fitting in or filling the mold that was crafted in the minds of others. How does a girl fit in when she doesn't even know who she really is? From childhood to adulthood aimlessly trying everything to fit in, but no success. Then one day I discovered Proverbs 18:16 and it changed my life.

This scripture let me know it was ok to be me. I could be authentic and didn't have to subscribe to the status quo. I could be me! The dynamic, uniquely and awesomely made woman that God had created me to be. I had gifts that would lead me into my greatness and put me in rooms that I never dreamed I would be in.

Never in a million years did I think I would live the life of an educator. I had dreams of being on the road as a promoter in the theater industry. Then I took a spiritual gifts assessment and I scored high in teaching. I thought I would just teach children's church and theater in church. But, as we all know God had different plans for me. As an educator I always felt like I could not reach the goals that were set for me, until I realized my style was for my students and not my observers.

I realized that God had put me in the classroom to be a leader and to pour more than 'book' knowledge into my students. Being in the classroom also prepared me for where I was going in the future. I learned compassion and most of all giving someone multiple chances when they were not their best towards me. Let me tell you I was the type you only had one time to do me wrong and I was cutting you off completely. I made up my mind at a young age that someone only had one time to hurt me. I guess you can say that was my way of protecting myself. God was using my gift to make room for me. I kept working and eventually my style was recognized as being what the population I served needed. As my gift developed more, I saw other gifts emerge.

I began to see my gifts of empowerment, motivation and inspiration emerge that I never knew I had. I began to lead girls groups, women's workshops and write my first book. The trajectory I was on made me feel like I could conquer the world. I just get moving in the grace that was allowed to me and doors began to open for me locally, nationally and internationally. I was walking in the favor that God had granted to me.

Who knew that girl who felt like no one believed in her or wanted to hear her voice now being heard. With all of the low self esteem not feeling like I was good enough. Was standing strong on:

Proverbs 18:16 A man's gift makes room for him,

And brings him before great men. (NKJV)

In order to fully embrace it I made it personal and intentional:

- Deborah's gift makes room for her,
- And brings her before great men and women.

The power I needed when I made it personal and intentional empowered me immediately. I felt like I could conquer the world. That nothing I put my mind to do I couldn't do especially with the God on my side. In that instance emerging from an extremely dark place this was the fuel I needed to power all of my cylinders to move forward and come out of my depression, self doubt, and feeling like a failure. Now I embrace life and all that it has for me. I know that God is setting me up for greatness and I'm ready to fully walk in it. I am embracing the visions that God has given me. I don't know where it's going to lead me, but all I know is that God has given me the gifts needed to reach to the highest heights and most of all acknowledge Him in all I do. As long as I trust Him with all my heart, soul and mind. And give Him glory with all of my gifts.

Affirmation:

I will utilize my God given gifts in all that I do. He wants to see me prosper as the leader that I was created to be. I know that my gifts will make room for me. I'm worthy of success.

Deborah Franklin

Deborah Franklin works with high achieving women to increase their VIP (Visibility Influence Profits) by telling their stories. Deborah is the owner of Deborah Franklin Publishing (DFP) and the founder of Church Girl CEO and Church Girl CEO Foundation. Deborah has a heart for women to expand their mindsets past what they can see. As a survivor of verbal abuse, she has learned to rise above what has been said to her and about her to be the authentic representative of who she is created to be.

Deborah Franklin is the author of 'adjective,' '21 Days 21 Minutes of Prayer & Meditation,' and "#5 30 Days of Motivation & Inspiration,""The Prayer of Jabez In The Marketplace," podcast host of Conversations w/Deborah Franklin and a media coach. Deborah has been working as a media coach for several years with clients who are authors, speakers and entertainers.

Deborah also uses her platform to give other aspiring talents an outlet to let their talents shine. Her ultimate goal in life is to help others to ignite the power within to propel them to their destiny while walking in their destiny.

Application\Notes

How will you apply this verse to your life?

Unleash the Revolution of Protection Through Disaster

By Erica Quarles

Psalm 91 Turned my life around indefinitely, for so many reasons. First, we as people should learn the armor that our Almighty Father above has equipped us to apply in our spiritual lives on a day-to-day basis to defend us from evildoers and the deadly snares of the enemy. Becoming a Minister in Evangelism I have had to protect myself from the raging wars of this world, mentally and physically. When Satan knows the word that God has put in you to deliver, he will rise against us more. For we do not wrestle with flesh and blood but with the rulers and the principalities of darkness.

Hearing as well as seeing in the spiritual realm, Psalm 91 has helped enhance my gifts to use this as a weapon of defense. This scripture of all the scriptures, has proved to me over again how our Father God lives and walks the earth. How He has plans to protect us and keep us safe from hurt, harm or danger. Equipping ourselves to use God's word for our everyday lives is so important. How can people learn about God? Well, we can learn by accepting Christ as our personal Savior. Taking the necessary time to get to know God for yourself can help you to determine which scripture is needed to use in every situation that should arise.

    Secondly, humbling ourselves under the mighty hand of God can help us from the attacks of the enemy. This scripture changed my life because we have to be prepared to fight. After all, Satan comes at us to kill, steal and destroy. He has attacked my family, my marriage, my money, and my health. The only thing I had to stand on was the living word of God. I learned that instead of fearing Satan, to utilize the defense that is brought against him and the other demonic spirits. It taught me to have confidence in God and believe HE does have my very best interest at heart.

    This scripture has protected me from diseases, evil, and any plaques coming near my tent. When we know the word of God, we can stand on it. God loves that we take the time to read about him. When we use his promises, he will abide by them. Moreover, when we utilize faith, this is when God's words come into motion, we must believe so we can receive. What I learned is we have to speak God's language to him. Most people believe in what they can see. Strengthening my relationship with God is the best way I choose to live my life. Knowing God more intimately will change your life forever. Because HE has surely changed mine. Anytime, I have to go to a place to swim with sharks, which means people who are not of God, this very scripture has cleared the pathway of any evil illness or plague. The best thing I could have done was to get to know God for myself.

Erica Quarles

Erica Quarles, is an Early Childhood Educator and owner of, E's to Bee's Daycare. For the past nine years, I've had the joy of nurturing and educating young minds in a loving and supportive environment. I'm thrilled to share that I've been accepted into the Early Childhood Undergraduate Program at Notre Dame of Maryland, where I will complete my Bachelor's Degree and obtain my teaching certificate.

Beyond my professional life, I am a dedicated Minister of the Gospel, a loving wife, and the proud mother of three wonderful boys.

My passion for early childhood education and my commitment to my family and faith are the driving forces behind everything I do. Thank you for being a part of our journey at E's to Bee's Daycare!

Application\Notes

How will you apply this verse to your life?

Empty Vessels, Fulfilled Blessings

By Amy Philpott

How many times have you reread a scripture that you knew as a child and may have still been very familiar with the story as an adult, but when you read it this time, it just hits differently? Your eyes opened, your heart opened, and you saw yourself in that scripture.

The wife of a man from the company of the prophets cried out to Elisha, "Your servant my husband is dead, and you know that he revered the LORD. But now his creditor is coming to take my two boys as his slaves." 2 Elisha replied to her, "How can I help you? Tell me, what do you have in your house?" "Your servant has nothing there at all," she said, "except a small jar of olive oil. 3Elisha said, "Go around and ask all your neighbors for empty jars. Don't ask for just a few. 4 Then go inside and shut the door behind you and your sons. Pour oil into all the jars, and as each is filled, put it to one side." 5 She left him and shut the door behind her and her sons. They brought the jars to her and she kept pouring. 6 When all the jars were full, she said to her son, "Bring me another one." But he replied, "There is not a jar left." Then the oil stopped flowing. 7 She went and told the man of God, and he said, "Go, sell the oil and pay your debts. You and your sons can live on what is left." 2 Kings 4:1-7 NIV

I had been enjoying the full time mamapreneur life since 2018, but for most of 2023, for some reason, I really struggled spiritually in seeing what value, if any, that I was bringing to our family being home. Between unexpected large expenses, my social media accounts getting hacked and taken down with over 10 years of my business content completely gone, trying to rebuild my business now from scratch, and my personal health declining with doctors not being able to provide any answers, it felt like my world was crashing down around me. At one point, I just sat in my car and cried. But being a mom of 4, being alone doesn't last long. My youngest son, Sam (who was 6 at the time), jumped in the front passenger seat wearing his Ninja Turtle costume toting a cup of ice. I asked him to leave so I could be alone. He refused saying "Mom, if I'm here, the devil can't get you. You're tired, scared, hungry, and alone. You are giving him full access to you! So if you want to sit here and eat your ice and take a nap go ahead. You don't have to be scared (proudly and confidently pulling out his toy katanas, bō, sais, and nun-chucks), I've got this."

It was at that moment, my heart started to slowly change. I taught Sam that over a year ago. He not only remembered it, but knew exactly how to apply it. I was a long way from seeing my value, but it was the spark that I needed to get started. It wasn't until I joined a 21 Day Prayer Challenge in January of 2024 that I really started to see God working and my heart changing. Holy Spirit revealed this truth:

When you don't see the value in what you have, you will never receive the blessing that is to come from it.

This woman likely thought Elisha was off his rocker with his request. Sometimes being obedient to God just doesn't make sense to us, in that moment. Something in her made her and her sons do this. God was asking her to pour what little she had into vessels that were more empty than she was. Her faith allowed God to amplify and multiply what little she had into something that was more than enough. The blessing only stopped because the jars ran out. God provided more than enough to pay off this woman's debt. It was enough for the family to live on! They went from slavery to salvation in her obedience.

I humbled myself, became transparent and I asked my prayer challenge group and my warrior friends to join me in prayer to open my eyes and to change my heart. Holy Spirit started placing scripture stories on my heart with similar themes as this one. In Matthew 14 we learn about a boy who offered to share his food of 5 loaves and 2 fish when the disciples were trying to figure out how to feed the 5,000 people. This boy saw the value in what little he had and offered it to Jesus. The Lord amplified and multiplied it to not only feed the 5,000, but had 12 baskets of leftovers! We see a similar story again in Matthew 15! In 1 Kings 17 we read about Elijah trusting God to feed and take care of him. Then immediately after, God worked though Elijah to do even more than that for a destitute widow & her son. She obeyed Elijah and made him a biscuit with what would have been her

& her son's meager last meal. God again multiplied something so small and saw to it that they never ran out of flour & oil again.

God opened my heart to show me that when I started questioning my choice to stay at home, I was really questioning Him. My belief in Him didn't shift, my trust did. My spirit had become empty like the widow's vessels. As I started each day doing chores, I would ask Holy Spirit to refill my heart with the joy that had quietly exited my spirit. Through prayer, worship, and our daily talks, it didn't take very long for me to start being refilled with this joy. It's funny how when I started to trust Him again, my attitude changed and so did the rest of my family. Everyone was more helpful and grateful, even at the smallest of things. When I chose to trust Him with what I valued, He amplified and multiplied it. I trust that He will continue to bless it. I'm off to get more vessels.

Amy Philpott

Wife, mom, teacher, volunteer, prayer warrior, The Queen of Bling, all of these titles could be used to describe Amy Philpott, but the thing that people see through all of these hats and titles is her spirit of servanthood and love of her family. Amy's passion is to show women how they can stay home, raise their kids, and run a successful home business with their family. It is possible to have it all, she is living proof. Together they work their family business.

This family dynamic approach has earned them much recognition and multiple advancements. Amy also retired from her longtime corporate career at the age of 40 to raise her children and focus more on Wayside Gems. Amy resides in Shelbyville, TN with her husband, Benji and their 4 children: Frank, Clara, Sam, and Nora.

They are members of Fair Haven Baptist Church and serve in several areas of ministry.

Amy also volunteers at her children's school assisting in reading fluency as well as Running Club. She is also serving on the Board of Directors for Church Girl CEO and is a 20+ year member of the Order of the Eastern Star. For fun, the family likes to help out on their mutli-generational century farm, camping, swimming, and anything with Scouting BSA. Born and raised in the suburbs of Chicago. She earned her degree in math and science from Grand Valley State University in Allendale, MI.

Contact Information:

On the web: waysidegems.com

Facebook: facebook.com/thewaysidegems
facebook.com/WaysideGemsVIP

Instagram: waysidegems

Email: thewaysidegems@gmail.com

Application\Notes

How will you apply this verse to your life?

My Plan vs. God's Plan

By Pixie Lee

When we are children, we often play games that "predict" the future. We know what profession we want to be in and most of us chose to be a doctor or a lawyer. We know how many kids we want, where we want to live and even what kind of car we want to drive. But as we grow older, our lives begin to shape into the first version of the adults that we become. Some of these things that we chose as children, we do accomplish, but most of the time, all of this is different.

Growing up as a PK or preacher's kid, during my middle school and high school years, I just wanted to fit in. I didn't want anyone to know that my dad was a preacher because by this point, I was sick of all the jokes and had literally heard them all. No one was original and as you can guess, none of them were funny. I was hanging with crowds that were doing things I didn't even want to do, again I just wanted to fit in.

As life continued to happen, I embarked on several journeys. I became a mother at a young age and got married at a young age. I had to go to school at night because I worked during the day, now that I had more responsibilities and a family to provide for. I could no longer hang out with my friends because I had children at home that were depending on me. I also got a divorce at a young age.

While on my path to "find" myself, I started relying on my religion and relationship with God. I started asking certain questions in an attempt to find myself. I started my second business but this time, I wanted to be connected with other people who weren't afraid to talk about their relationship with God. I still wanted to fit in, but I wanted to fit into a different crowd. I asked God to connect me with other entrepreneurs on the path I was on but had him at the center.

I remember going back to my bible and reading the popular scriptures. The ones you learned and memorized in vacation bible school and Sunday School. While it was helpful to get the scriptures back in my spirit, but the scripture that hit home for me the most was Jeremiah 29:11 NIV "For I know the plans I have for you, " declares the Lord, "plans to prosper you and not to harm you, plans to give you hope and a future."

Reading and hearing that scripture was so comforting and eye opening. It put my life over the past couple of years into perspective. Even though I've had some challenges, this scripture told me that it was all a part of the plan that God has for my life. God knew I was going to walk this path, and I would get to this point. Everything that has happened both good and bad had to happen. It was unavoidable.

We always want to avoid the bad and only acknowledge the good, but that's not reality. The bad is what builds faith and builds character. The bad is what helps you to know God is with you. The bad is what confirms God has never left you. So, when I hear and read Jeremiah 29:11, it's comforting for whatever situation I am dealing with. It gives me hope for the season that I'm in. I know that this is all a part of God's plan.

Pixie Lee

She hails from the Big A! Pixie was born and raised in Atlanta, GA, and was educated in the Cobb County School Systems. She obtained her degree in Accounting and began her entrepreneurial journey in 2010 by opening her Accounting and Tax firm. After things slowed down, she returned to Corporate America while still running her firm on a part-time basis. That was the first time she would hear the words "life coach". She was met with a health crisis that changed her focus and the staple incident that would forever change her life. After being at her job only 2 years, she went through her first-ever layoff and found herself at a crossroads in her life. Still trying to determine her next steps, she recalled 2 different conversations where 2 of her co-workers spoke to her that she should become a life coach. She's always been the go-to person for advice and had a great listening ear. At that time, she wasn't sure because she didn't want to go back to school though. Thinking of the extended amount of time in classes and of course a growing student loan balance, she had more questions than she did answers.

After sitting still and researching, she found a class and became certified in 1 day. It was still a tall task now to build her business. But, she didn't want to build her business the traditional way so she wrote her first book, "The Power of Purpose." She had always dreamed of writing a book but was never sure what the book would be about. After hiring a book/writing coach, within 4 months, her book was done. She had become a published author and penned The Power of Purpose.

Her book opened doors and connected her with people who have been instrumental in assisting her to build a life coaching business. Looking to expand her business and use her gift for words, she became a ghostwriter and coined the phrase "I Got All The Words." In 2020, she released her second book; Forgiveness is Key, but she had something bigger brewing. Watching the world react to the pandemic God told her it was time for the people of God to hear from the people God had called. She spoke with her father and finally convinced him to become a published author himself. Her publishing company, PL Publishing was born, and her first collaboration was An Anchor for The Ages.

With her foot on the gas, she entered the world of television with her business partners Kandie and Deborah forming KDCP Network. It was formed to give a voice to female entrepreneurs to show the world that women can work together successfully and create a platform to talk about any and everything women deal with in business, ministry, family, and much more.

She is the editor-in-chief of The Believer's Ladder Magazine. A quarterly magazine that talks about ministry and entrepreneurship and gives hope and motivation to those on the path to change the world. They are changing the way we do and see ministry with every issue.

Adding another layer to her ever-changing resume, she has partnered with Inspired By You and runs the therapeutic writing program. Together they are not only helping to heal those who are suffering from traumatic events and trauma, but they are also creating new published authors.

When she's not working and writing, Pixie is a mother of 3 and a grandmother of 1. Family is everything to Pixie. It's her goal to publish 50 new black authors. Pixie lives by the mantra "If she takes care of God's people, God will take care of her".Pixie Lee

Application\Notes

How will you apply this verse to your life?

Entering His Rest

By Wendy Dailey

Have you ever watched a hamster run on the wheel in his cage? He runs and runs until he is exhausted and worn out. It doesn't matter how fast he runs, when he is tired and reaches his destination, he always gets off at the same place he began. Nothing changes and he cannot figure out why. Despite how many times he runs or how fast he runs, there is no progress and his position remains the same. He remains locked in a cage, running in circles, going nowhere fast. This cycle summed up my life. I worked hard, raised my children, and tried to be there for others. I supported my children with all their endeavors, supported friends and family with their accomplishments, and spent countless hours assisting others at church. I ran around and did all these things but neglected to pursue an intimate relationship with God. As a Christian, I believed it was my duty to help and make sacrifices for others and there was no way I would make it to heaven without serving in my local church. It got to the point where I was exhausted, empty and unfulfilled. I prayed and asked God for direction but couldn't hear His response nor discern what direction to take to improve my life. I couldn't understand why it was so easy for others to hear the voice of God while I struggled. As a result, I continued to run on the hamster wheel while pretending to be happy .

I will never forget the morning I finally heard God speak to me. He said, "Take My yoke upon you and learn from Me." I was so excited to finally hear from my Father. I immediately reached for my journal to record the words that would change my life. I knew that what I heard was part of scripture, therefore I searched for it so that I could develop a revelation of what the Lord was saying to me. Matthew 11:29 says, Take my yoke upon you, and learn from me, for I am gentle and lowly in heart, and you will find rest for your souls."

Take My Yoke Upon You

A yoke may be considered an emblem or symbol of subjection, servitude, slavery, etc. God's desire for his children is to take his yoke but that was not what I did. I was enslaved to yokes of religion and rejection and they were reigning in my life but I couldn't see it. I knew that I was saved by grace, but I lived in bondage to man's rules and good works for years. I knew that I was accepted by the Father, but the rejection I endured throughout my life blocked me from embracing his acceptance as well as other benefits of salvation. The harsh reality was that I lived as if I were an orphan or one who had no Father. I began to read my Bible, spend time in the presence of God, and confess scripture over my life. As time passed, I began to hear the voice of God more clearly and the yokes of religion and rejection began to be replaced with Jesus' yoke. I will admit that I have not arrived but I know that my Father loves me and accepts me. I don't have to earn his love or attention.

Learn From Me

Since the beginning of my walk with God, I listened to many sermons and read a lot of books but did not sacrifice time to spend with Him due to busyness. The Father was not interested in how many times I went to church or how many books I read. He desired to reveal himself to me and to show me the identity he had given me. I realized I was not acting as a child of God. I was living as an orphan who had no Father or place to call home. I quoted many scriptures centered around being a child of God and living a kingdom life but they were not rooted in my heart. I did not possess a heart of sonship. The yokes I had taken on caused me to see the Father as a Master instead of a loving Father. I was independent, self-reliant, and convinced that I could not trust others. After spending an extended amount of time fasting and praying, my love for the Father became more pure. I became interdependent. I started to trust Him and others that he placed in my life. God began to teach me about Him. I began to view life's challenges as a way to learn from Him instead of punishment for the things that I have done. As I continue to learn from him, my love for Him and others increases.

For I Am Gentle and Lowly In Heart

The Father has the purest heart to ever exist. One encounter with His gentleness captivated me and I willingly surrendered my heart to him. As I continued to surrender my heart, I began to see his humility and I wanted to be like him. My heart, which was occupied with offense, pride, rejection, fear, and deep-rooted pain, began to be filled with love, humility, acceptance, and trust. As He continues to reveal the areas of my heart that need his healing, I push through the pain and surrender. I now understand why it was so hard to hear the voice of God. I had too many blockages!

You Will Find Rest For Your Souls

To rest means to cease from action or motion; refrain from labor or exertion; and to be free from anxiety or disturbance. Rest for my soul means to be free from the things that separated me from developing an intimate relationship with God. I no longer rely on others for acceptance or love. I chose to get out of the hamster cage to embrace a love like no other, that is the love of my Father.

Wendy Dailey

Born and raised in Florida, Wendy Dailey graduated from Florida Memorial University with a BS in Elementary Education. She is a devoted mother to four children. She enjoys family and loves to spend time with her grandchildren. When she has time, she likes to steal away to the beach to read and enjoy the serene ambiance. She is an experienced teacher who is passionate about developing strong readers. She has received extensive reading training through a multi-sensory approach called Orton Gillingham. This approach has equipped her to help students who were not able to learn to read through other approaches. As an upcoming graduate from Nova Southeastern University, she hopes to broaden her ability to ensure that children can receive the reading instruction that is ideal for their unique needs. As an aspiring author, Wendy hopes to educate and motivate others to move beyond life's challenges and limitations.

Application\Notes

How will you apply this verse to your life?

Who am I, and where did I come from?

By Ethel J. Davis

And, "I will be a Father to you, and you will be my sons and daughters, says the Lord Almighty." 2 Corinthians 6:18

Have you ever felt so different that you felt like an alien? Perhaps you felt like a stranger within your own family? From a young child, I felt odd, awkward, ugly, and disconnected from a worldly perspective. My childhood was a two-parent household, along with two older siblings. We grew up in a faith-based environment where we attended church every Sunday and went to vacation bible school in the summer months.

My mother's side of the family consisted of four sisters and one brother. Most of her siblings resided in Wichita, Kansas, and were part of a close-knit group. We all attended the same church on Sundays, and after church, we would have fellowship and break bread together at someone's residence. I loved all my relatives but had a special bond with my mom's youngest sister – Beatrice Williams. She was my favorite aunt, and I spent many summers with her, and she taught me so much about life. Her children were grown with families of their own. Therefore, many of her grandchildren were my age. However, I did not find that we had many common denominators, so those relationships were simply surface-level connections.

Beatrice (aka Aunt Bea) was the first formal entrepreneur in the family, and she had her own salon where she styled hair for many clients. She was a beautiful woman who wore stylish clothes and had the most beautiful jewelry in the world. While it was never verbalized to me, I realized later that my low self-esteem issues were a priority to her. She would style my hair, allow me to experiment with her nail polishes, and dress up in her beautiful clothes and jewelry for fun. She was so lovely, classy, successful, and loving that I wanted to grow up like her. Yet, something kept holding me back because a void kept clinging onto me – no matter what I did.

Throughout my formidable years, I continue to "battle" with that low-hanging dark cloud. I found the nerve to ask my father if I was adopted because I did not look like any of my family members. My father hesitated with his response and told me to discuss this matter with my mother. However, I did not approach the subject with my mother, for I felt it would make her feel uncomfortable with my questioning of my existence. She told many stories about my birth and the little things that made my birth special.

This silent volatility in my life continued until I became a teenager when something drastically changed my outlook on life. Everyone has a family member who drank too much adult Kool-Aid, and their mouth becomes a lethal weapon. Regrettably, that individual was my mother's brother, who asked if I would ever look for my biological parents. His mouth moved slowly, but his words did not match his tone. He started by asking what were my plans after graduating from high school. Then, without a transition statement, he asked if I was curious about finding my biological parents. Why was he asking me about my biological parents? I only remember feeling sick, shocked, and discombobulated regarding the content of his conversation. Of course, I ran to my parents in horror, screaming what was he talking about – biological parents. The blank stare, confusion, anger, and silence made me realize he had struck a nerve with my parents. Before they began to speak, I knew it was true because it took them too long to respond to my questions. Why would they keep such a secret for so many years? Of course, my mind was swirling with so many thoughts of blackness, for who am I? Where did I come from?

My parents called all my siblings together and started to unravel the history behind our family's infrastructure. My mother's voice was very deliberate, and she confirmed the adoptions were truthful and that we were adopted individually to become a collective family. What? I remember feeling sick because my entire world was a fairy tale. Everything about my birth was a lie? She said, "I was adopted at five days old from the University of Kansas hospital." My mother and father attempted to have children immediately after their marriage. Unfortunately, it was not happening, so my mother went to the doctor to try to understand why they could not conceive. They ran tests and could not find anything wrong with my mother's reproductive health. Eventually, they turned to my father and discovered it was his problem, and they could not have children. Yet, my mother's number one priority was to have children. She was not going to give up on her dreams, so she convinced my father that adoption was the compromise for this unforeseen turn of events. We all had a closed adoption, and they did not want anyone to reference us as their adoptive children.

Once, alone in my bedroom, I cried out to God about the dark cloud looming over me from an early age. Who would give up their child to strangers? Why me? Who am I, and whose blood runs through my veins? Plus, I had to think that while I had siblings, we were not blood-related. How did they feel, and would they reject me from being their little sister? I considered only myself and could not imagine how they thought about this new reality. Yet, I heard an internal voice that said, "God decided in advance to adopt us into his own family" – Ephesians 1:5 (NLT). I believe it was a sermon from God advising me that I was chosen and sought after as a daughter to my parents. Adoption is a blessing from God, but it took some time to resonate with my heart and soul. Eventually, I thought God loved me long before I came. He had shown favor in my life for desperately bringing two people who wanted children. Finally, I decided it did not matter who my biological parents were because my past was not going to limit my future. I got to the point where I celebrated all the parties for their role in my life. In fact, I hope that the two people who conceived me have peace within their souls that they did the right thing – no matter their circumstances. I felt an insurmountable peace and joy that God was not holding anything against me, for I am HIS beloved daughter.

Some people may refer to me by a derogatory name, but God calls me his daughter. Plus, I realize everything happens for a reason, and I walk by faith, not sight. Still, I am grateful that God knew my name long before I came to be a reality. He sent Vergie and Zether Davis to choose me from all the other babies that were up for adoption. I do not chalk that up to luck – it's favor. God makes things happen for a reason and a season, and I finally feel complete. I did not choose my entrance into the world. God did. He was elevating me to a higher level and wearing my blessings unapologetically.

My gratitude to my parents is my legacy. I named my Registered Investment Advisory firm VZD Capital Management, LLC after them. I aimed to pay homage to the two people God sent to raise me as their daughter. Therefore, in adopting us, God gives us the very Spirit of his Son and grants us to feel the affections of belonging to the same family of God. With each passing day, I want to reflect God's love for me by being intentional about what I do. The bottom line is that I do not want to come up short when the day comes when he calls me home. However, I want the world to know my gratitude to God for bringing me the right parents who raised me to be who I am today.

Honoring one's mother and father is essential for my life today and always.

Ethel J. Davis

Ethel J. Davis, a recognized wealth manager, has over 36 years of experience within the financial and investment arena. She is the CEO and Chief Investment Officer of VZD Capital Management, LLC, a Registered Investment Advisory firm in Lenexa, Kansas. In 2012, she founded the company, a legacy namesake for her parents – Vergie and Zether Davis. Ethel's parents are deceased, and she continues applying the values and principles they instilled in her, inspiring her daily work. For instance, her father's emphasis on integrity and her mother's dedication to service is reflected in every decision she makes for her clients. Her firm serves affluent individuals, multigenerational families, Trusts, and non-profit organizations, and she is committed to providing them with the highest level of service and care.

Ethel, a proud small-town woman from Iola, Kansas, is honored to be the first African American woman to own 100% of a Registered Investment Advisory firm in the Midwest and a few within the United States. Her expertise is widely recognized, as she is known as a Five-Star Wealth Manager, acknowledged by the Kansas City Business Journal as one of 20 Financial Professionals You Need to Know (2023), a member of the Kansas City Business Journal Women Who Mean Business, a KC Magazine Business Magazine Influential Women, and a 2024 Top Black Women to Watch by the CIO Magazine. This recognition in the industry is a testament to her unparalleled expertise and dedication.

Ethel believes her most outstanding achievement is serving others with grace, humility, and servitude. She has also given many accolades to her mentors – Cleo Brager, Karen Herman, Patrick Callaway, and Michael Dayton. She is family-oriented and proud of her bonus children—Melissa Geist, Melinda Seamster, and Michelle Boyd—and her two bonus grandsons, Avion Seamster and Alex Giest. She is grateful to her sister Helen for being so generous and unselfish in sharing her children with her so she did not miss out on motherhood. Ethel has mentored many women and men throughout the Greater Kansas City Community and chose Nikisha Johnson as a "baby" sister she never had. She is also the Senior Vice President of VZD Capital Management. Ethel's values of faith, family, and service drive her work, inspiring others to follow their own path with courage and determination and serving as a beacon of inspiration in the industry.

Application\Notes

How will you apply this verse to your life?

"Trusting in God's Providential Care"

By Rev. Jackie "Lady J" Miller

Psalm 121

A Song of Ascents.

I lift up my eyes to the hills. From where does my help come?

My help comes from the LORD, who made heaven and earth.

He will not let your foot be moved; he who keeps you will not slumber.

Behold, he who keeps Israel will neither slumber nor sleep.

The LORD is your keeper; the LORD is your shade on your right hand.

The sun shall not strike you by day, nor the moon by night.

The LORD will keep you from all evil; he will keep your life.

The LORD will keep your going out and your coming in from this time forth and forevermore.

I have talked about my Grandmother in other publications. Honestly I was this old when I realized how influential she has been in my Christian development, my walk and my overall belief in God. I come from a background of Pastors, Preachers, Deacons and Evangelist so I was fully exposed to the Word of God, but my Grandmother was truly the most influential.

Psalm 121 is not only my favorite scripture but for as long as I can remember it has been my go to scripture because growing up whenever I communicated with her, in my teenage through adult years, she would always tell me to read "Psalm 121". In fact, she gave me the first bible that I can officially remember, regarding that I could read for myself was one of those small New Testament Psalms and Proverbs (Pocket Size Bibles) that she had marked the scripture as a reminder for me to read. Ironically enough, I still have it although my eyes have aged and I can't see it. But it serves as a reminder for me to keep my foundational scripture at the forefront of my mind.

I grew up leaning on this scripture. Not really understanding the impact it was going to have on my life later. You ever find yourself in a strenuous situation and the first thing to mind is a scripture that you have been taught all your life.

"I will lift up mine eyes unto the hills, from whence cometh my help" really became my help early on in my life. I truly learned that God was my help when I allowed myself to be infatuated with a young man who worked at a gas station near my home. I'd see him when I would go get gas on my way home from my part-time evening job. Somehow I ended up in a back room in the gas station and he was pressuring me to be intimate. Until this day I can't recall how I got back there. This was one of the many times in my 57 years of life that I am so grateful for God's Providential Care.

I can remember so clearly one of the many times God answered me after calling on Him through this Psalm. Out of nowhere someone showed up, needed something that took quite a bit of time, which allowed me time to escape possibly being raped. It was then that I knew I was His. God saved me once again. At that time in my young life that was the only scripture that I could remember off the top of my head. Sure I had grown up in church, went to Sunday school, and had been baptized, but in that moment of crisis that's what I could recall.

Many nights and days I have cried out to God. Giving Him back His words, reminding Him that He said, my help comes from the LORD, He would never slumber nor sleep and that He would keep me from all evil. He has kept His word!

Psalm 121 gives me immense comfort when I'm in the midst of life's storms. Over the years I've had my share of many ups and downs

One of my biggest struggles though, is worrying. Worrying about that which I have no control over. We all do it, at some point in time we have been crippled by worrying.

Yes, Worry can be crippling; In spite of how or who has raised us, or our belief, we still worry. I am guilty of trying to have control over everything. So I used to spend a lot of time worrying about what I could or couldn't do, should or shouldn't say, go or not go.

It took me a long time to understand that there's absolutely nothing wrong with being careful, cautious, and prepared, but I don't need to be in full control, full control will always be out of my reach so stop worrying about that which is out of my control. And it's okay, actually it's a good thing, because it points me to the one who is and I am reminded who I really need to seek and allow to have ALL control.

There are few things that unite all people in life, regardless of our religion, race, culture, language, habits, weight, height or even the size of our bank accounts… one of those is WORRY!

But for me when I remember to "Look to the Hills where my help comes" I feel better. The "hills" are symbolic of God, The LORD who is My Keeper, my provider, my protector, my way-maker, my healer, my guide and the source of my strength.

The world wants us to live in fear of what is or what is to come. However, I see Psalm 121 as a beautiful poem that reminds me of what I somehow keep forgetting, I do not have to live in fear, because I have a daddy in heaven, my God who keeps me and protects me, and not only me but my family too. I realized a long time ago this scripture not only changed my life, it has saved my life repeatedly.

Today, I am a grandmother of eight and I have already started teaching my oldest grandson Roman who is seven years old, Psalm 121 because I know one day it will come to be his protection and source of strength as it is mine.

Jacqueline B. Miller

"Lady J"

Is a creative; energetic multi-facet Woman of God. Answering "the call" she feels is by far the greatest accomplishment of her life. As an ordained Minister of the Gospel, a Couples Coach, Life Coach, Writer, Published Author and Virtual talk show personality you will find that she has a servants' heart, loving and caring for God's people is the fundamental foundation she stands on.

Lady J, is the creator and founder of the show, Victory Talk, which is heard across the internet, she finds so much joy in helping others in learning to #Speaklife and share their accomplishments as they grow to their next level. She does her best to fulfill her desire to motivate and inspire others to live a Victorious Life. **Lady J's** initiative and determination keeps her focused. Her resilience is her primary motivation to glorify God and her edification of others.

She and husband Pastor Phillip A. Miller, Sr. of Victorious Living Faith: Not Your Traditional Church work diligently to bring about change in the lives of God's people and communities. **Lady J** has a passion for marriages and helping couples to grow while keeping the fires hot! Along with her husband they have been leading the "Yes Marriage Works; If You Work It" ministry for over 16 years.

As Co-Pastor of VLF she prefers the background where she can encourage and serve God's people with complete anonymity. Overall **Lady J** is very comfortable leading from the second chair.

Jacqueline's most humble service to God has been as a wife, a mother of six children and grandmother of eight grandchildren. She believes living the example before them, is her most challenging yet rewarding mission in life.

CONTACT: Jacqueline B. ~Jackie "Lady J" Miller

On the web: http://Vlfminstrys.org/

Facebook: @ victorytalk
or https://www.facebook.com/jackie.y.miller

Twitter: @JackieLadyJ1

Instagram: JackieLadyJ1/ Jackie Miller

Email: speaklifeladyj@gmail.com

Lady J

"Don't allow your past to rob you of your future"
...I can do all thigs through Christ who strengthens me...Philippians 4:13.

If you have Faith, nothing shall be impossible for you...Matthew 17:20

Application\Notes

How will you apply this verse to your life?

Broadening Your Perspective

By Dr. Yvette Harris

The two of them could not get the mattress up the steps. As I watched them struggle, I remembered the homework assignment my pastor gave us that Sunday. Say your favorite scripture throughout your life during the week. Would it really work for two men to get a mattress up a flight of steps? Father, You said that if I call on you that you would answer me and show me great and mighty things that I know not. Jeremiah 33:3. Their next attempt to get the mattress upstairs was successful. Two men who were not believers, got a mattress of the steps after I spoke the Word. While there were various times during that week, I said that verse, it was that evening in 2003 that I remember.

I don't recall how I was introduced to the verse; however, I do know that I first heard it in 1991 soon after I became a believer. Outside of Psalms 23 and John 3:16, Jeremiah 33:3 was the first verse I memorized it after becoming a Kingdom Citizen in 1991. Why does this verse mean so much to me? Because no matter what I am going through, what I need or desire, or even how I feel; this verse reminds me and solidifies how much the Most High cares about and loves me. In Scripture his verse does not have a specific context. For example, it has nothing to do with the fruit of the Spirit, healing, earthly possessions, troubles or anything specific. It is, however, the word that was given to Jeremiah while he was in prison. Definitely a good time to call on ABBA!

After that week in 2003 this verse stayed and continues to stay at the forefront of my life. Whether I am driving down the highway needing to get through traffic or getting a report from a doctor. I know that I can call on the Most High, that He will answer me and show me great and mighty things that I do not know in every situation at all times. The Message Version creates an amazing image. It reads, "Call to Me and I will answer you. I'll tell you marvelous and wonderous things that you could never figure out on your own." We hear a lot about standing on the promises in the Word. We know that there are thousands of them. This verse is a promise. Yahweh says, He WILL answer when we call. That just means we must call on HIM. We don't have to perform, and there is no condition attached. That is truly a Kingdom promise! That's love from our good, good ABBA Father – our Father who is our SOURCE! Recently, this verse became my life.

Between October 2022 and May 2024, I had a major crisis experience along with an extremely exciting change occur in my life. On October 3, 2022, my beloved daddy; my best friend, strongest supporter, and confidant would unexpectedly make his transition to heaven. He was not ill and had no medical conditions. Throughout the next year, I called on Yahweh daily. Because of the relationship I had with my daddy, this was new to me. It was new to me because I struggled on an almost daily basis interchanging, the Father and my daddy is first in my life. I know that's not the right thing to do, but it was my reality. It was Jeremiah 33:3 that helped me navigate a grieving process, and ultimate transformation into my new and exciting life. There were days that I struggled to do anything productive, but I called on my Heavenly Father with every expectation that He would answer. I called on the Most High and he sent ALL the help I needed while he healed my heart. Along the way, there were people that helped me with things. Some of which I knew that I needed, and some I did not. It was during this period that I learned how to ask for help. In learning how to call on Him because I no longer had my earthly daddy, I learned how to ask for help from others. The verse was living and breathing in my life. As time moves on and my heart healed, I began to see the Yvette I longed to see. A smile that was real. Managing life and all its nuances better than I ever had. I also began to see dreams and visions that I had written come to fruition.

In December 2023, I embarked on the homebuying process. I Had attempted to purchase a home several times between 2016 and 2022, and again in 2023. Each time was unsuccessful. On December 2nd, what would have been my daddy's 90th birthday, I began the process again. This was unexpected, because I planned on waiting until after the new year. This time, the process took two days for loan approval. That was just the beginning. For the next five months things would happen and at times I did not think I would move into my dream house. Two weeks prior to closing escrow I was informed I needed to come up with a large sum of money. I let the lender know that I did not have the money. When I hung up the phone Jeremiah 33:3 was part of my prayer. A week later, the amount of money was reduced by thousands. And at the close of escrow, a good portion of the money that I borrowed from someone was refunded and paid back before I moved in June 11, 2024.

No matter what your circumstance, or who you may have to deal with, call unto the Most High, He WILL answer you, AND show you great and mighty things you do not know. Jeremiah 33:3. It is a PROMISE from Him!

Dr. Yvette Harris

Dr. Yvette M. Harris is a seasoned educator and trainer with over 30 years of experience. After serving in the United States Air Force and working in corporate America, she began a career in the field of education. Her career in education, which has lasted 20 years, began as a classified employee. After developing a passion for providing a high-quality education for children, Dr. Harris would obtain her teaching credential. Her teaching career began with instructing adults seeking re-entry in the workplace. She also taught parenting teens who were academically deficient.

Throughout her career, Dr. Harris would work as a teacher, counselor, professional development coordinator, and an administrator. Her career has also allowed her to work in programs where she was responsible for assisting staff and administrators reform schools to meet the needs of struggling students. Dr. Harris has worked with schools to develop their school-wide State aligned curriculum and instruction programs, along with student discipline, and Career Technical Education programs. Additionally, these efforts also included writing and co-writing local, State, and Federal grants. She has worked with schools, districts, and County offices of education to secure funding from $5,000.00 to over $230 million dollars. Her work has been accomplished in both traditional and charter school settings.

Dr. Harris has worked diligently throughout her career to train both certificated and classified staff, faculty, and administrators. She firmly believes all students can learn and will utilize her network of resources to bring that vision to fruition. Her instructional career has also included serving as an online adjunct professor.

Education and Development Resources (EDR) Consulting Services, Inc. integrates the skills Dr. Yvette Harris implemented in her work over the last 30 plus years. She is a professional trainer and educator with superior writing and communication skills. She is also an Internationally certified John Maxwell trainer, coach, and speaker and a certified DISC behavioral analysis trainer. EDR trainings are designed for diverse audiences. The EDR team maintains a high level of professionalism whether working with an individual client, or in a boardroom with a large audience. Their commitment to developing cooperative relationships is passed to her clients by listening with intent to assist and focus on what the client is requesting.

EDR's trainings and written works are grounded in cultural competency and social justice. The workplace is diverse and training should be designed to meet the needs of all in attendance. Because Dr. Harris has real world work experiences from being an entry-level employee to working in upper management capacities, she possesses the unique ability to tailor her trainings and relate to the entry, mid, and upper level employee. The EDR team is committed to providing excellent training to all clients and seeks to ensure trainings reflect those qualities.

Application\Notes

How will you apply this verse to your life?

Committing to His Plan through your Pain

By Tracy Shorter

My life changing moment happened the first weekend in October 2018. At this time, I was an active event planner, and my schedule was packed with multiple events. When my pastor called a corporate fast for that same week, I wondered how I was going to manage the schedule and keep my energy up too. But it was important for me to participate, as my business and personal life was at a crossroad and I was seeking clarity around PURPOSE.

That Sunday morning, I was getting ready for worship service, but my physical body was tired. However, my spirit was just full of energy, looking back it was the strangest of things. The first song had ended and halfway through the next one, which was "Total Praise", I began to feel strange. My eyes were blurry, and I looked at my friend, another Traci in my life, for help. However, I couldn't get my thoughts together to speak and then everything went black. Now most of the members in the congregation figured it was a "spiritual moment", but I was told later that my face went almost ash gray, so those around me knew something was wrong. After being checked by medical personnel, my heart rate was low and I had a nasty headache. Since I already had irregular heartbeat issues and still was on the corporate fast, I just figured I needed to eat, take my medication, and get some rest, so I went home.

My daughter insisted we call the doctor the next morning, who instructed me to come in for a check-up. On the way to the appointment, my phone beeped with a text alert to my morning devotional prayer. A gentleman's voice begins to recite *Jeremiah 29:11: For I know the plans I have for you," declares the LORD, "plans to prosper you and not to harm you, plans to give you hope and a future. In the New Living Translation, it says, For I know the plans I have for you," says the LORD. "They are plans for good and not for disaster, to give you a future and a hope.* I had heard this scripture before and as the man talked, I felt comfort. We arrived at the doctor's office, and she performed the exam, scheduled a CT scan, and made some medication modification(s). I went back to life as usually, believing that with some rest and time, my body would bounce back.

As I was finishing up my midweek workday, the phone rings. The nurse practitioner informed me the doctor needed a few minutes to go over my test results. The CT scan had found a PseudoTumor Celibri. I was going to need to see a neuro-ophthalmologist as soon as possible. And so, for the next year, I saw several doctors who created treatment plans to deal with the vision struggles and the daily headaches. As I was adjusting to the treatment plan and trying to manage my full-time job, plus my event and travel business - my mind was all over the place. How could Jeremiah 29:11 be true for me? *Was my future really going to be good?* I learned that if you have questions and you ask the Holy Spirit expecting an answer, then answers are what you get, but they may not always be the answers you want to hear.

But I needed a settling of the mind, so I went back to my scriptures seeking such an answer. I started with Jeremiah because I remember the comfort I felt the day I heard the devotional prayer.

As I researched the back story of Jeremiah, I then understood the full meaning of verse 11. Jeremiah was a prophet speaking to a group of people who for a long period of time were going to have various hardships. The word he was giving from God was to remind them and us that good plans don't necessarily equate to things being easy - that bad things will happen even to those who believe and trust the Lord. Yet we MUST remember to NEVER give up because there is hope in the future that we can't see. That reminded me of Proverbs 3:5-6- "Trust in the Lord with all your heart and lean not on your own understanding. In all your ways submit to Him and He will make your path straight. "

You see, I was having many of the symptoms before I received the doctors' call, but the moment I received the call, the symptoms had a new name other than "I'm getting older." I stopped trusting and believing in a future that was going to be good. It was now the third weekend in February, and had taken me four (4) months to realize that

I had to stop questioning the plan and instead put my trust in my plan builder.

Jeremiah 29:11 is that perfect reminder to us that life is like working with a builder to build a house. It will be messy, can come in over budget, have project delays and even sometimes the plans must make a complete pivot to start all over again. However, by applying Proverbs 3:5 to make God your builder, you can be assured to walk in the promise of Jeremiah 29:11. It was that weekend that I decided I was going to change the words coming out my mouth. I would continue to believe for total healing from Pseudo Tumor Celebi. It could be a quick process or it could take some time, but in the meantime my future is bright. My builder has created a plan and while it's a good one, it's not without challenges, regardless I am not to take my eyes off the end results.

Tracy D. Shorter

Whenever you interact with Tracy Shorter one thing for sure is going to happen, you will leave encouraged, supported and have a new cheerleader in this journey we call LIFE! With a strong servant's heart and over fifteen years of strategic planning experience, she has been helping others fulfill their vision and create memories through planning travel adventures, live events and her non-profit work under Tracy Shorter Enterprises. Then in 2016, the Lord spoke the word BELIEVE to Tracy. Unbeknownst to her, she would need it more than ever in 2018, when an unexpected health forecast came without warning. After months of prayer, the message was clear simply- BELIEVE! It was not just a direct word to Tracy, but that she was to spread that message to others around her and a new purpose unfolded for her to help others live life to its full potential.

To reach Tracy:

Tracy D. Shorter

Tracy Shorter Enterprises

www.tracyshorterenterprises.com

tracy@shorterenterprises.net

Application\Notes

How will you apply this verse to your life?

_____
_____
_____
_____
_____
_____
_____
_____
_____
_____
_____
_____
_____
_____
_____
_____
_____
_____
_____
_____
_____
_____
_____

www.ingramcontent.com/pod-product-compliance
Lightning Source LLC
Chambersburg PA
CBHW060659030426
42337CB00017B/2697